Snapshots in Time

Photographic Memories of Puget Sound

Kathleen Thompson

Book Publishers Network
P.O. Box 2256
Bothell • WA • 98041
Ph • 425-483-3040
www.bookpublishersnetwork.com

10 9 8 7 6 5 4 3 2 1

Printed in the United States of America

LCCN 2015938475
ISBN 978-1-940598-69-7

Editor: Barbara Kindness
Cover designer: Laura Zugzda
Typographer: Melissa Vail Coffman
Production: Scott Book

I dedicate this book to my two sons, Steven and Douglas, that you may know your grandfather and great-grandfather a little better and remember them a little longer.

Love, Mom

This is the story—through pictures—of one family's early business venture in Seattle. Price Photo Service provided employment as well as a love of photography to several generations. Were it not for their abiding interest in the growing city, many views of days long past would be lost, or at least minimal.

It began with my grandfather, Albert E. Price, who was born April 8, 1873, in Elmore, Nebraska. In his earlier career, Albert managed the H.P. Curtis Company, maker of shirts, pajamas, and robes. But from 1921 to 1924, he entered into a partnership—Price and Carter, Commercial Photographers and Amateur Finishers, located at 518 Crary Building in Seattle, Washington. Price and Carter became Carter and Bradley Photo Co. in 1925. Albert also managed the photo lab for Eastman Kodak and was a commercial photographer.

In 1925, Albert opened Price Photo Service at 7315 Greenwood Avenue, in North Seattle. My dad, Donald, inherited Grandpa's interest in photography, and while stationed in Attu, Alaska, in the US Navy during World War II, he would fly over the coast of Japan photographing activity there, then return to the lab in Alaska and process the films to forward to the appropriate officials to keep them updated!

Shortly after Dad's return from the Navy in 1945, Grandpa passed away so my mother, Doris, and my grandma, Mae, took over the running of Price Photo Service. Dad continued the long-standing working relationship with Eastman Kodak Company too.

Joe, the first delivery driver for Price Photo Service

I was number four of six kids in our family, and I had the wonderful experience of working at Price Photo beginning about the age of nine. What a thrill it was to receive my first paycheck for the summer in the amount of twenty-five dollars. I would accompany my dad into the darkroom, which was totally black with the exception of one yellow safety light. Here he would process 35mm film. I listened as he opened each canister, removed the film, clipped the top of the film onto what looked like pants hangers, and clipped a weight to the bottom of each roll. This process continued until all canisters were open and ready to be submerged into the tall tanks (they were about as tall as my dad) and set below the level of the floor so he could easily reach the top of each tank—first the developer, then a rinse, then a stop bath and another rinse, each carefully timed. This completed the processing. He would then take them into the main shop area and hang them under large dryers mounted to the ceiling blowing warm air down onto each roll of film. When dry, they would be cut and prepared for the person doing the printing.

I watched as my parents and a few other staff completed their parts, carefully entering a number for identification for each order, exposing the paper with the image from the negative. Then they placed each picture into the developer tray and carefully watched until the image was clear and complete. Carefully, by hand, each picture would be placed in a basket on the rocker, which would rock back and forth in a steady motion to completely rinse each picture. After the developer was rinsed off, the baskets would be raised and the pictures flipped into the next bath, first the stop bath and so on into about five different baskets. There was a dark curtain that the rocker passed through allowing the pictures into the light for the first time. This is where my job began! I carefully placed each picture on the dryer, a large, heated, mirrored roller that moved on a canvas conveyor belt (also called the apron). If the photograph was printed on glossy paper, I placed it on the apron face-side up to the mirror; if it was matte paper, it would be face down. Being very careful to place each picture straight, I would watch as they traveled around the large drum. There was another basket placed at the end of the rotation of the hot drum. Hopefully each picture would drop off at the appropriate time. If not, I would carefully lift a corner of the hot photograph allowing it to fall into the basket. From there, all pictures were sorted, counted, and priced then placed in a completed envelope for each customer.

We had walk-in customers at our shop and also a pickup and delivery service that consisted of my grandmother and me. During summer vacations, I rode with my grandmother, and we would do the route, consisting of several businesses located in Green Lake, Northgate, Ballard, Magnolia, and West Seattle. I would run into the store delivering the completed orders from the day before and pick up the new ones. This very well may have been the first one-day photo service! Grandma continued her work at Price Photo Service until the age of eighty!

I never met my grandfather, Al Price, as he passed away before I was born. But I grew up knowing what he stood for:

> *With faith and love in God, life is full, loving,*
> *and meaningful.*
> *There is always room for one more at the dinner table.*
> *Family takes care of family, and family is forever.*

I am so very grateful to him for the many beautiful pictures he took, cherished, and passed down that now are being shared in this book. I am also grateful to Grandma Mae for diligently creating many photo albums, adding the date and location whenever possible. Dad tried desperately to keep Price Photo Service running by himself; however, it was not meant to be. He sold Price Photo, accepted a position at Boeing where he quickly became head of the photo lab, and later enjoyed retirement.

May you enjoy this brief photographic journey through Seattle's yesteryear.

Downtown Seattle and Lake Union, looking north.

Hotels, restaurants, apartments, and a variety of small businesses bring new life to downtown Seattle (early twentieth century).

St. James Cathedral, a designated city landmark in First Hill neighborhood, was first built in 1907.

Looking down on Yesler Way from the
forty-second floor of the Smith Tower, June 1921.

Second Avenue, early Seattle.

Seattle's historic Triangle Pub, originally a hotel and bar, was built in 1910.

Elliott Bay with the Smith Tower, long before skyscrapers.

Seattle's train station dates from the early 1900s.

Stewart & Holmes Drug Co. (foreground) was started in 1886 with locations in Seattle, Tacoma, and Walla Walla.

Schmitz Preserve Park, a favorite of hikers and nature lovers, has over fifty-three acres of old-growth forest and walking paths on Alki Point in West Seattle.

Beautiful statuary in Tacoma's Wright Park, a twenty-seven-acre arboretum and public park with hundreds of plant species.

A wintry scene on Second Avenue from Union Street with Bartell Drugs, the oldest family-owned drugstore chain in the nation, in right foreground.

Unpaved Second Avenue was a bustling hub of activity with the popular Hotel Savoy standing between Seneca and University Streets.

View from the top of the Arcade Building, ca. 1913, which stood on the west side of Second Avenue, between Union and University Streets.

Snow covered the Arcade Building, which was finally torn down in the 1980s.

A downtown Seattle streetcar on a wintry day at Second and Union Streets.

H. H. Watkins and other shoppers brave the cold and snow to visit such stores as F. W. Woolworth Company, one of the original five-and-dimes.

Creativity had no limits on Seattle's snowbound downtown sidewalks.

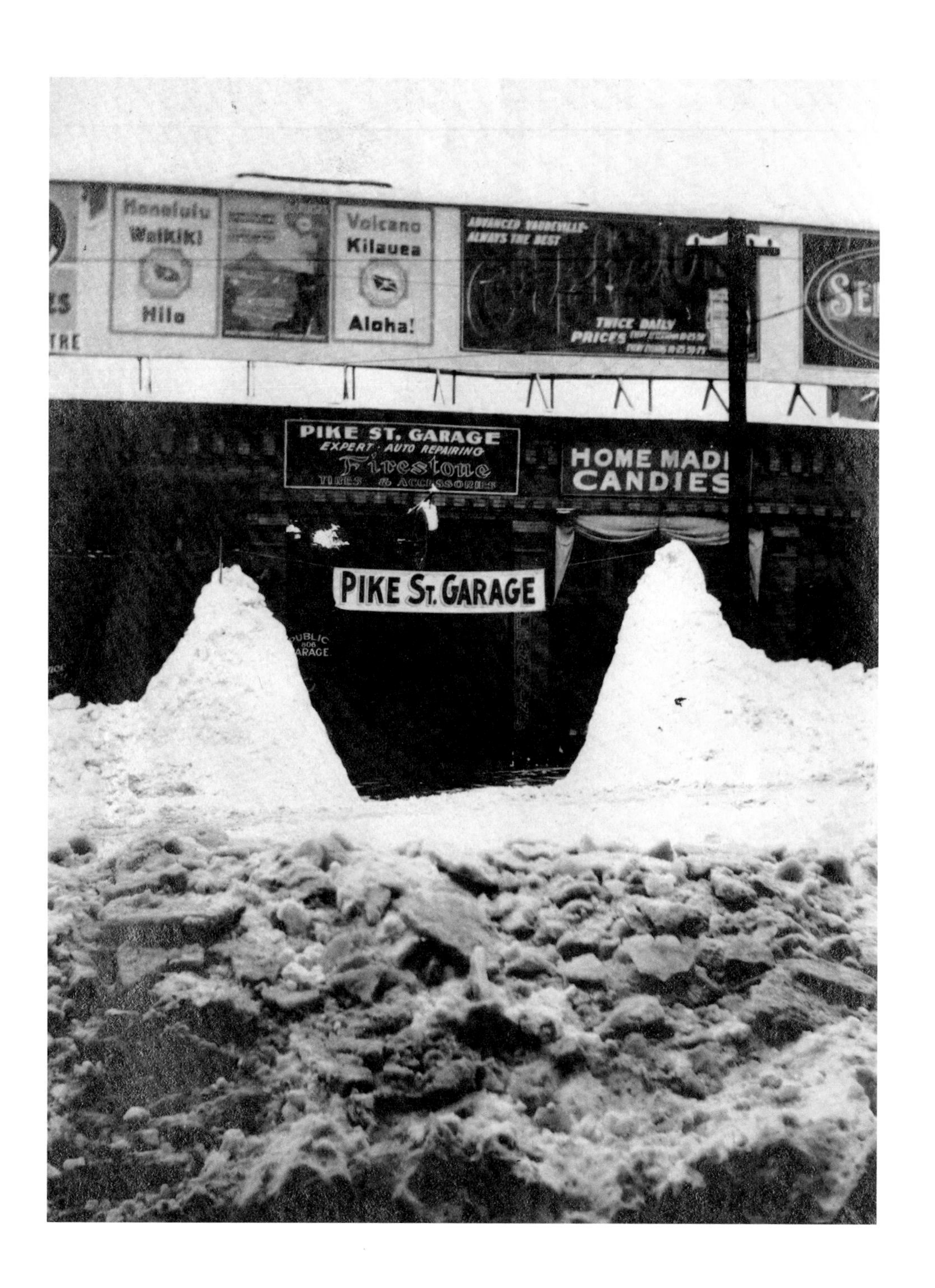

Snow, snow everywhere, between Eighth and Ninth Avenues on Pike Street.

Joe's Place, across from the post office at Third Avenue and Union Street.

The Liberty Bell in Seattle, ca. 1915.

Japanese Pagoda Lantern, Mount Baker Park.

Denny Hall's Varsity Bell was brought to Seattle from Troy, New York, around Cape Horn in 1861–1862.

Wild West Parade, a popular attraction year after year.

Native Americans in the annual Wild West Parade.

The touring Al G. Barnes circus began in 1895 and by 1929 had grown to five-ring size.

Snow-covered roof of the Arcade Building.

Construction of the Burke Building (on right), on the northwest corner of Second Avenue and Marion Street, was begun in 1889, but the Great Fire that year in Seattle's downtown business district delayed completion until 1891.

Looking down on snowy Second Avenue from the Arcade Building rooftop.

Renton car line at snowbound snowbound Fourth Avenue and Union Street stands in front of three attached early high-rise office buildings (White, January 1909; Henry, September 1909; Stuart, January 1915).

The Coliseum Theatre at Fifth Avenue and Pike Street opened in 1916 as the first Seattle theater built specifically for movies.

Frink Park in Seattle's Leschi neighborhood is heavily wooded.

Building boom in Seattle.

The Smith Tower, opened in 1914, was once the tallest building west of the Mississippi.

The Smith Tower's Chinese Room and observation deck on the thirty-fifth floor offer breathtaking views of Seattle and an unforgettable venue for weddings or other special events.

A bustling city keeps developing uphill from Elliott Bay.

The ship embarks on its maiden voyage.

Ship launch draws an excited crowd.

The Ballard end of the Hiram M. Chittenden Locks, a link for boats between the salt water of Puget Sound and the fresh water of the Ship Canal, which connects to Lake Union and Lake Washington.

The Hiram M. Chittenden Locks.

The canal locks, named after US Army Major Hiram M. Chittenden, were formally opened July 4, 1917, and added to the National Register of Historic Places in 1978.

Ford's Model T assembly plant was built at the south end of Lake Union in 1914.

US government hulls line Lake Union.

Green Lake, a favorite recreational area in Seattle for skating in the early twentieth century and for biking, jogging, walking, boating, and swimming today.

South end of Seattle's Green Lake.

North end of Seattle's Green Lake.

Volunteer Park Water Tower, at an elevation of 520 feet, is the highest point on Capitol Hill with a fabulous 360-degree view of Seattle.

The falls at Denny Blaine Park.

Lake Washington Boulevard above the Leschi neighborhood.

Parades through downtown Seattle with dignitaries always drew a welcoming crowd.

Parade on Second Avenue in downtown Seattle.

Military unit marches in Seattle parade.

Military marching band.

A. Baker clearing snow in Volunteer Park.

Seattle's snow-covered Volunteer Park.

Seward Memorial in Volunteer Park honors William H. Seward, secretary of state under Abraham Lincoln and Andrew Johnson, who arranged the purchase of Alaska (called "Seward's Folly").

Volunteer Park, designed by renowned landscape architect Frederick Law Olmsted, features a historic conservatory and the Seattle Asian Art Museum.

Looking down at the flower beds from atop the Water Tower, Volunteer Park.

Entrance to Cowen Park, formed when melt-off from the Vashon glacial ice sheet formed Lake Russell and cut drainage ravines. Today, a favorite playground and picnic site.

Ravenna Park, along with Cowen Park, comprises a single contiguous recreation and green space just north of the University of Washington.

Stately residence in Capitol Hill neighborhood, situated on a steep hill just east of Seattle's central business district.

Home in Rainier Valley. South of downtown Seattle, the neighborhood has the single most diverse zip code in the United States, evident in its Vietnamese, Ethiopian, Somalian, Middle-Eastern, and Asian shops.

Crowd gathers to see master escape artist Harry Houdini dangling from the Seattle Times building in a straightjacket, 1915.

Leschi Park. The well-manicured grass, exotic trees, and flowers belie a turbulent history as the campsite of Chief Leschi of the Nisqually tribe.

Mount Baker Park, designed to be a quiet neighborhood park near Lake Washington, was so named because of its view of the majestic Mount Baker, one hundred miles north.

Alki Beach, a favorite sunbathing and swimming area off West Seattle.

Alki Point Lighthouse, with its thirty-seven-foot octagonal tower, was completed in 1913.

Sunset on Puget Sound.

A wintry sunset.

Alki Point Lighthouse.

Ships at sunset.

A beautiful sunset along the Pacific coast.

Sunset on Lake Washington.

Steamship Tacoma *served from 1913 to 1938 on Puget Sound.*

The Duwamish, *constructed in 1909, was the world's most powerful fireboat, a record held for ninety-four years.*

The steamer Minnesota *in Seattle's harbor, ca. 1909.*

Navy ships in Elliott Bay.

Navy battleships in Elliott Bay.

Tree-lined entrance to the University of Washington campus.

Denny Hall, originally built in 1894, is the oldest building on the on the University of Washington campus.

The sundial on University of Washington campus was a graduation gift from the class of 1912.

Blethen Chimes, University of Washington, arrived about 1912.

Swans on a pond at the University of Washington.

The Forestry Building, one of the earliest buildings on the University of Washington campus.

Massive Denny Hall, named for Seattle pioneers Arthur A. and Mary Denny, sits on the highest point on the University of Washington campus.

Engineering Building, University of Washington.

Formal gardens and promenades surround the Music Hall built for the Alaska-Yukon-Pacific Exposition in 1909.

Woodland Park Zoo was established over a century ago in 1899.

Seattle waterfront from a viaduct at Marion Street.

Winter along the Seattle waterfront.

Wreck of the steamship Admiral Watson *in Elliott Bay, 1915.*

Denny regrade.

The convict ship Success *was on exhibit around the world for over fifty years.*

Forms of punishment for prisoners.

Snoqualmie Falls, one of Washington's most popular scenic attractions, is on the National Register of Historic Places.

Snoqualmie Falls.

Monte Cristo and the Cascade Mountain Range.

Traveling to Monte Cristo on the Hartford Eastern Railway.

Glacier Falls above Monte Cristo, a favorite for hikers.

Monte Cristo, now a ghost town in eastern Snohomish County, was the first live mining camp (for lead and silver) on the western slopes of the Cascade Range, ca. 1895.

Eagle Park in Mount Rainier National Park.

Narada Falls, in Mount Rainier National Park, is 188 feet (57 meters) and has two tiers, with Mount Rainier Highway crossing between them.

Mount Rainier.

Mirror Lake at the base of Mount Rainier.

Tahoma Glacier on the western flank of Mount Rainier.

View of Mount Rainier from Indian Henry's Hunting Ground.

Paradise Inn at Mount Rainier, the most popular spot for visitors to the park.

Longmire Springs in Mount Rainier National Park was named for James Longmire who built cabins and trails in 1883 around the hot mineral springs, visited by hundreds of people every year.

The Tatoosh Mountain Range runs along the southern boundary of Mount Rainier National Park.

Cascading falls.

Longmire Springs Hotel, originally a five-room hotel built in 1890, was expanded and by 1906 had thirty rooms.

Cabins crowded under evergreens in bygone days.

Mount Rainier.

View of Mount Rainier from Indian Henry's Hunting Ground.

Mount Rainier.

Wildflowers and towering trees surround the road to Mount Rainier.

Mount Rainier: natural beauty from every angle.

Visitors to the park.

Creek near Monte Cristo.

Cabin dweller in the shadow of Mount Rainier.

An eagle soars above the American flag
(cover of Pacific Marine Review *magazine, July 1918).*